COMPETITIVE
TRACK AND FIELD
FOR GIRLS

CLAUDIA B. MANLEY

the rosen publishing group's
rosen
central

Published in 2001 by The Rosen Publishing Group, Inc.
29 East 21st Street, New York, NY 10010

First Edition

Library of Congress Cataloging-in-Publication Data

Manley, Claudia B.
Competitive track and field / Claudia B. Manley.
p. cm. — (Sportsgirl)
Includes bibliographical references and index.
ISBN 0-8239-3408-X (lib. bdg.)
1. Track—athletics for women—Juvenile literature. [1. Track and field. 2. Track and field for women.] I. Title. II. Series.
GV1060.8.M36 2001
796.42'082—dc21

2001000752

Manufactured in the United States of America

Contents

Introduction   5

1. An Introduction to Track and Field   10

2. Training   21

3. Competition   42

4. Opportunities for Track
      and Field Athletes   47

Timeline   50

Glossary   54

For More Information   56

For Further Reading   58

Index   61

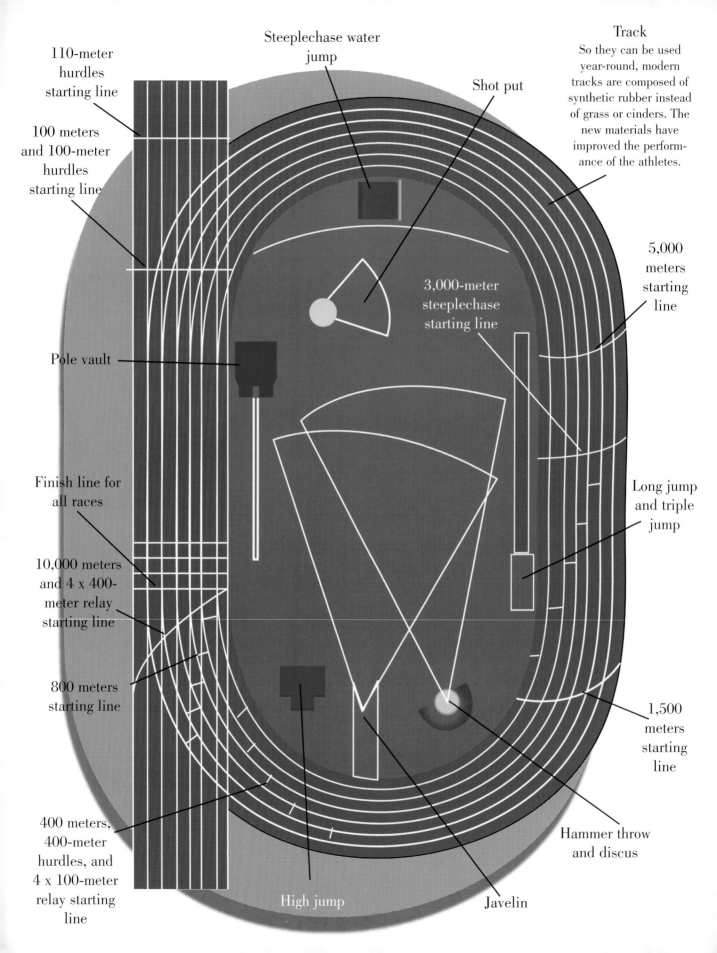

110-meter hurdles starting line

Steeplechase water jump

Shot put

Track
So they can be used year-round, modern tracks are composed of synthetic rubber instead of grass or cinders. The new materials have improved the perform-ance of the athletes.

100 meters and 100-meter hurdles starting line

5,000 meters starting line

3,000-meter steeplechase starting line

Pole vault

Long jump and triple jump

Finish line for all races

10,000 meters and 4 x 400-meter relay starting line

800 meters starting line

1,500 meters starting line

400 meters, 400-meter hurdles, and 4 x 100-meter relay starting line

High jump

Javelin

Hammer throw and discus

Introduction

There's no definitive record of the early days of track and field, but pole vaulting is said to have debuted at the Tailteann Games in Ireland in 1829 BC. There's also a mention of an event similar to the shot put that occurred during the siege of Troy in 1100 BC, when the soldiers had a rock-throwing contest. One of the hallmarks of long-distance running, the first official marathon was run at the Olympic Games in 776 BC.

Women were not allowed to participate in early Olympic Games. Married women were forbidden to even attend. One woman, Callipateira, had to dress as a trainer so she could see her son compete. When she forgot herself in excitement over her son's win, she revealed her true identity. The Greeks thereafter required all athletes and trainers to strip before entering the stadium so that no other married woman would sneak in.

Women and the Early Olympics: The Heraea Games

This sculpture of the Greek goddess Hera was carved in 490 BC.

The Sixteen Women, a council made of representatives of each city of the ancient state of Elis, hosted a competition for maidens (unmarried women) every four years. These were held in honor of the Greek goddess Hera. These games consisted of footraces staged among maidens of the same age.

They used the same stadium at Olympia where the Olympic Games were held but cut the distance of the field by one-sixth. The youngest women ran first, followed by the next oldest, and so on up to the oldest group. While the games did not have the prestige of the Olympics, they were still respected by the Greeks. Winners of the races were given crowns of olive leaves and a portion of the cow that had been sacrificed to Hera.

England is credited with the development of track and field events as they are practiced today. As early as AD 1154, practice fields for track and field events were set up in London. It is claimed that King Henry VIII was a very good hammer thrower.

The 1800s saw the sport spread. The first North American meet was held near Toronto, Canada, in 1839. In the 1860s, the New York Athletic Club was formed and held the first indoor meet, while in England, the Amateur Athletic Club was founded and held the first English championship. Track and field became truly international when the Olympics were revived in 1896.

However, female athletes have not had the same opportunities to compete as men. The International Amateur Athletic Federation, founded to govern international track and field events in 1912, didn't include women's events until 1936. Athletic opportunities were limited for girls in the United States until Congress passed the Education Amendments, which included Title IX, in 1972.

Title IX deals specifically with discrimination against girls and women in federally funded educational institutions. It didn't make a big impression or cause controversy when it was first passed. In fact, guidelines on how to enforce it weren't even issued until 1974, and even then little was done to enforce it. In 1984, Title IX took another hit when the Supreme Court said in the ruling for *Grove City v. Bell* that schools didn't have to follow Title IX guidelines in programs

The women's Olympic track and field squad posed for this photo as they left for Europe on the SS *Manhattan*, on July 15, 1936.

that didn't receive federal funding directly. This included athletic programs.

This ruling outraged women, who lobbied for broader inter-pretation of the amendment. In 1988, the Civil Rights Restoration Act was passed. This stated that sex discrimination was against the law in any educational institution receiving any federal funding. So even if the school's athletic program didn't receive federal funds, but another program did, the sports pro-gram still had to follow Title IX's guidelines.

Title IX means that schools must provide equal funding and resources to female athletes as they do for male athletes. What does this mean for you, the female athlete and budding track star? It means that the kind of money provided for a boy's team must also be provided for a girl's team.

Many female Olympians and professional athletes credit the passage and enforcement of Title IX for their success in sports. It has also provided athletic opportunities for thousands of "regular" girls as well.

1

An Introduction to Track and Field

As many as twenty-five different events make up a track and field meet. Women's track events generally include the 100, 200, 400, 800, 1,500, 5,000, and 10,000 meters; 100- and 400-meter hurdles; and 400- and 1,500-meter relays. Some meets may include longer relays as well as marathon and race-walking competitions. Field events can include high jump, long jump, pole vault, triple jump, shot put, and discus, hammer, and javelin throws. In addition, athletes may compete in the heptathalon, a cumulative seven-event competition. To participate in track and field, you don't need to be able to do all of these sports. The great thing about track and field is that there is an event for almost every kind of athlete.

Equipment and Cost

All track and field events require shoes that grip the track or launch surface and protect the foot while still being lightweight. You should select shoes that fit well and perform under your event's conditions. Other equipment you might invest in could be a javelin, a vaulting pole, or any of the other throwing implements. The cost of these items can range anywhere from $30 up to $250 or more.

Many schools have track and field teams; however, they may not field a team that competes in all events. If you can't find a team at your school, check with USA Track and Field or Athletics Canada to see if there's a recreational youth team you could join.

An official outdoor track is a 400-meter (440 yards) oval. The actual track surface can be dirt, clay, or crushed brick. All major competition tracks have surfaces made of synthetic materials. These provide better and more consistent footing in all weather conditions. Jumpers and javelin throwers also

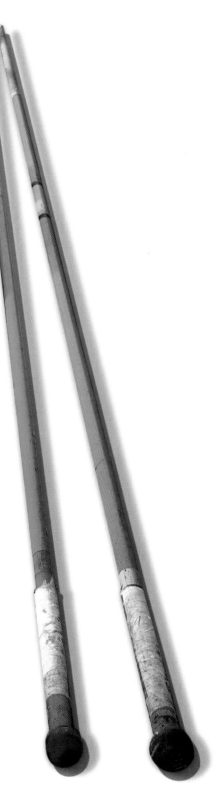

Javelins like these are used in track and field.

An official outdoor track is a 400-meter oval and can be composed of dirt, clay, or crushed brick.

compete on a synthetic surface, while athletes in the shot put, discus, and hammer throws use concrete circles. Indoor tracks range in size from 150 to 200 meters (160–220 yards) and have a synthetic surface over wood. Cross-country events use any available terrain, including roads, parks, and golf courses.

Track

If you're quick and can use all of your energy in a relatively short burst, then sprinting may be your skill. A sprint is a race up to 400 meters. A sprinter performs at top speed from start to finish.

Thousands of spectators attended the first day of the track and field competitions at the 2000 Olympic Games in Sydney, Australia.

All runners must have their hands and feet on the track at the start. Starting blocks (rigid supports for the rear foot) help runners get a quick start. They are required for races up to and including the 400-meter run. Runners are staggered; that means that they start at different points on the track to equalize the distance to the finish. The track is an oval, so the outside lane is longer. A sprinter in the outside lane (the one farthest from the center) will start slightly farther up the track. Runners must stay in their lanes, except in races longer than one lap. The runner whose torso (body) crosses the finish line first wins.

In hurdling, the runner must leap over gates that are three to four feet high while sprinting as fast as she can.

Mid-distance runs (those between 800 and 2,000 meters) require both the quickness of a sprinter and the endurance of the long-distance runner. These events also require a good understanding of race tactics like pacing, which allows you to save just enough energy to sprint to the finish.

If you have the power to run for a long time, then the long-distance runs—races longer than 3,000 meters—could be your events. These require less speed but more pacing and endurance. They are rarely finished with the kind of sprint you see in mid-distance runs.

The marathon is the longest race of a track meet and is 42,186 meters, or 26 miles and 385 yards (commonly referred to as 26.2 miles). It was one of the main events of the first Olympics and is named for the legendary run of a Greek soldier in 490 BC, who ran from Marathon to Athens to bring news of a Greek victory over the Persians. It was also a key event when the modern Olympics were revived in Paris in 1896.

Hurdling combines a sprinter's speed with the agility to jump over a series of obstacles called hurdles. The 100-meter high hurdles consist of ten hurdles that are forty-two inches high and spaced ten yards apart. The 400-meter intermediate hurdles also have ten hurdles, but they are only thirty-six inches high and spaced 38.29 yards (35 meters) apart. A runner may accidentally knock down hurdles during the race but will be disqualified if she uses her hand to knock them over. You don't want to knock them down as that breaks your stride.

The steeplechase combines hurdling with long-distance running. Over a 3,000-meter course, athletes must clear seven water jumps and twenty-eight hurdles.

Teamwork is essential for passing the baton in the relay event.

Because of its unique nature, athletes who run the steeplechase often only participate in this one event.

If you have speed, coordination, timing, and a good sense of teamwork, you might like the relay event. The two standard events are the 100- and the 400-meter relays. Relays have four runners per team and divide the running so that each girl runs 25 percent of the race. Passing the baton to your teammate requires coordination and timing on both the passer's and the receiver's part. A smooth and well-timed transition often makes the difference between a win and a loss. The 200-, 800-, and 1,500-meter relays aren't run as regularly.

Race walking is not always a part of a track meet although it is included in the Olympic Games as well as other multi-national events. In race walking, if both feet leave the ground at the same time, the walker is disqualified for running. Olympic distances are over 20,000 and 50,000 meters, but individual meets may set other distances.

Field

Field events fall into two categories—jumping and throwing. The four jumping events are the high jump, pole vault, long jump, and triple jump. The throwing events are the shot put, discus throw, hammer throw, and javelin throw. As of the 2000 Olympics in Sydney, women could compete in all field events.

The object of the high jump is to clear a thin rail supported by two stands. The jumper must leave the ground from one foot,

The pole-vault competition for women debuted at the 2000 Sydney Olympics. Stacy Dragila of the United States was the first woman to win a gold medal in the event.

not spring off from both feet. She can start at any height above the minimum set by the judges. As long as she doesn't miss three jumps in a row, she stays in the competition.

Jump techniques include the scissors, the western roll, and the belly flop. The most universally used technique is the Fosbury flop, named after 1968 United States Olympic champion Dick Fosbury: The jumper approaches the bar almost straight on, twists on takeoff, and goes over the bar headfirst, with her back to the bar.

The 2000 Sydney Olympics saw the debut of the pole-vault competition for women. Stacy Dragila of the United States was the first woman to win a gold medal in the event. As in the high jump, a pole-vaulter has three tries at each height to clear the bar. The vaulter races down a runway carrying a fiberglass pole. As she plants the end of the pole in a box sunken slightly below the ground, she pulls herself up and almost over the pole (like a handstand). As she nears the bar, she twists and arches so that her feet go over first and she is facing downward.

Speed is the most important element in the long jump. The runner approaches the takeoff board at top speed, plants one foot on it and leaps across the sandpit, often using a technique that looks as if she's running in the air. The jumper must make sure that no part of her leading foot extends beyond the takeoff board or the jump will be disallowed.

The triple jump was once known as the hop, step, and jump, referring to the three distinct segments of the event. Running toward the takeoff board, the competitor bounds off. She lands on the same foot she took off on and springs off of it. In the next motion she steps landing on the opposite foot and finally jumps into the sand pit.

In the shot put, the athlete "puts" a four kilogram (eight pounds thirteen ounces) metal shot that is about ten centimeters in diameter. The "put" is not traditional throwing; it's more like shoving from the shoulder. The arm cannot extend behind the shoulder. The putter (as the athlete is called) gets the momentum up by twisting rapidly inside the seven-foot shot-put ring. Shot putters are generally among the largest and strongest of the track and field athletes because of the strength that's required.

The discus throw is considered a classic event because of historical references in literature and art. Competitors launch a one-kilogram platelike disc from within a two-meter (eight feet two inches) circle after completing one and a half turns.

In the hammer throw, you don't really pitch a hammer. You throw a metal ball about 127 millimeters (five inches) in

You must have a strong upper body to shove the shot put from your shoulder.

diameter attached by a wire to a handle. The whole thing weighs around 7.26 kilograms (sixteen pounds). Holding just the handle, the thrower whips up centrifugal force by spinning around three or four times and then lets it fly. The launching area is just a little smaller than the discus throw area. Kamila Skolimowska of Poland won the first women's gold medal when the sport was debuted at the 2000 Sydney Olympics.

In the javelin throw, an athlete hurls a spear—a javelin—with all her strength. The women's javelin weighs at least 600 grams and is at least 220 centimeters long. This is the only throwing event that does not use a launching circle. The javelin does not have to stick into the ground to be valid, but does have to land with its point first.

Athletes can also participate in a multi-event competition called the heptathalon, which consists of seven events: 100-meter hurdles, high jump, shot put, 200-meter run, long jump, javelin throw, and 800-meter run. These competitions require a two-day schedule and are most often held at worldwide and national championships as well as college conference championships in the United States. Athletes are given points for their performance in each event and the one with the most points wins.

2 Training

Overall conditioning is important for all members of track and field. A good basic program should include cardiovascular endurance, strength training, stretching, and cross training.

Your heart's ability to deliver blood to your muscles over an extended period of time is measured by your cardiovascular endurance. Of course, track events require a strong heart whether you're a sprinter or a marathon runner, but many of the field events have running starts as well. Although the runways might be relatively short, think about how often you may have to run them if you successfully advance in a meet. It would be pretty disappointing if you didn't have the cardiovascular endurance necessary to make it to the runway for the deciding jump!

The lunge is a great exercise for building and increasing the strength of your thighs.

Any exercise that raises your heart rate and keeps it raised for at least twenty minutes benefits your cardiovascular system. You want to get that kind of workout at least three times a week. If you have track and field practice that often, you're probably set. Biking or skating are also good ways to condition your heart.

Strength Training

Strength training (also called weight training) is very important. Unfortunately some girls and women are afraid that if they lift weights they won't be as "feminine," or will become She-Hulks. Basic strength training will not only increase your strength but also give you a leaner body mass and less fat—quite the opposite of bulk! It can also give you a feeling of personal power, an ability to face many challenges and obstacles. Training with weights is also important for women because it helps strengthen bones. Women suffer from a higher rate of osteoporosis (bone density loss) than men, which can result in increased injuries from bone breaks.

Strength training should be done at least three times a week. Pay attention to your posture and breathing, and work your muscles smoothly. You can do most of the following exercises without going to a gym if you have free weights or dumbbells. Start with weights that require a bit of effort to lift but aren't so heavy that you can only do one set of repetitions. It's better to start lighter and increase weight than to strain your muscles trying too much too soon. Each exercise can be done in sets of fifteen for two or three repetitions. As soon as a weight feels light, switch to a slightly heavier one.

Quadriceps, Hamstrings, and Hips

A good exercise for the big muscles in your thighs is the lunge. Stand with feet parallel but slightly apart, a weight in each hand. Take a big step forward with your right foot without stretching or losing your balance. Slowly lower your left knee to the floor. Rise and return to the starting position. Switch legs and repeat.

If you do many repetitions ("high reps" in gym lingo) and use light weights, weight lifting will not bulk you up but will help you burn fat and look great!

Calves

To strengthen your calves, begin in a standing position with a weight in each hand. Slowly raise your heels till you are balanced on your toes. Hold for ten seconds. Lower yourself back to the starting position.

Shoulders

To do the shoulder shrug, start as before, with a weight in each hand. Raise your shoulders to your ears as though you were shrugging. Hold for ten seconds and release slowly.

Arms

The bench press is good for your arms and pectoral muscles. Lie on your back on the bench with your knees bent and a weight in each hand. Your arms should be bent with your hand resting at your shoulders. With a slow, smooth motion, push the weight away from you so that your arms are extended straight above your shoulders. Slowly lower them back down.

The bicep curl can be performed seated or standing. Hold a dumbbell in each hand with your palms facing outwards, back straight and feet on the floor. Slowly curl the weight toward your shoulders by bending at the elbows. Lower the weight slowly to the starting position. Repeat with the opposite arm.

For the tricep kickback hold a dumbbell in your right hand with the palm facing inward. Bending at the waist until your upper body is almost parallel with the floor, place your left hand on a bench or on your upper thigh for support. Bend your knees slightly and keep your stomach muscles tight.

Raise your right elbow and upper arm to the back, keeping your elbow tight to your body. Press the dumbbell backward, straightening your elbow until your entire arm is parallel to the floor. Hold briefly, then lower the weight. Perform one complete set, and then repeat with the opposite arm.

Stretching

Stretching helps make your muscles more elastic and increases your flexibility. Never stretch cold muscles. Warm them up with a light jog, by jumping rope, or by giving them a massage. A shower is another way to warm the muscles.

Here are a few exercises you can try. Make sure that you stretch the muscles and don't bounce. Breathe deeply and stretch until you feel a mild pull but no pain. Hold each stretch for fifteen to twenty seconds, rest for about ten. Repeat three times.

Calf Muscles

Stand about two feet away from a wall, a tree, or other sturdy structure. Step back about a foot with your right foot. Bend your left knee and lean toward the wall, keeping your back straight and your heels flat on the ground. Your right leg should be straight and you should feel a stretch in the right calf. You can move you left foot forward a bit to get more of a stretch if you need to. Return to the starting position and repeat with the opposite leg.

You should always stretch before any physical activity so that you do not injure your muscles.

Hamstring

Lie on your back and bring your left knee to your chest. Gently hold the back of your thigh with both hands and press your thigh into them. Keep the thigh muscle contracted and slowly extend your left foot to the ceiling until your leg is straight. Point your heel towards the ceiling. Keep the right leg extended, with the right thigh pressing down and toes pointing up. Switch legs and repeat.

Quadriceps

Face forward, bend your right knee, and grab your right ankle with your right hand. Bring your heel to your butt with your right knee pointing at the floor. You should feel a mild stretch along the front of your right leg. Hold this for twenty seconds and then switch legs.

If you don't have very good balance, get a partner to help. Stand face to face and balance each other by putting your left hand (when you're stretching your right leg) on your partner's right shoulder.

Inner Thigh/Groin

Sit on the floor, soles of your feet together, your heels at a comfortable distance from your groin. Holding your feet, place your elbows on your legs and bend forward slowly from your hips. Try not to round your lower back. You should feel a stretch in your groin area. As your muscles relax and this stretch gets easier, increase pressure on your legs with your elbows.

Shoulders

Raise your right arm. Bend it at the elbow so that your right hand is behind your head and your right elbow is pointing upwards. With your left hand gently pull your right elbow behind your head and toward the left. Let your right hand slide down your back. Keep your shoulders down and relaxed. When you feel the stretch, hold. Switch arms.

Cross training is a good way to stay in shape because doing different activities enables you to work your muscles in a variety of ways.

Cross Training

Cross training means participating in more than one sport. It gives you the opportunity to try something new. You will be amazed at how different an activity can be when you're not focused on competing.

Ride your bike leisurely, warming up for a few minutes. Then stand up and pedal as fast as you can for thirty seconds. Sit down and pedal slowly to recover and then try it again, maybe for forty-five seconds this time. Build up to one minute of this high-powered pedaling and then taper back down to thirty seconds. Cool down with a leisurely ride.

Yoga is an excellent cross-training option. Besides giving you increased flexibility, it also strengthens muscles and encourages you to focus on the moment. This frees your mind from obsessing about all those details that usually race through it. Walking and hiking are also good ways to cross train.

Injuries

Because track and field encompasses so many events, there are many opportunities for injury. We'll focus on some of the most common ones.

Stress fractures are small breaks in the bone that come from repeated stress and are most common in the leg bones (tibia, metatarsals, and fibula). Fractures in the foot bones are most common among sprinters and hurdlers. A sudden increase in the intensity of training (increasing how many miles you run), introducing a new activity (like hill training), a change of environment (switching from paths in the park to streets), and bad equipment (worn-out running shoes) all can contribute to stress fractures. Women are more susceptible to this type of injury if they have low bone density (osteoporosis), menstrual irregularities, or poor diets.

Basic treatment requires rest from the activity that caused the injury for about four to eight weeks. You can keep up your conditioning by cycling or weight training. It's important for

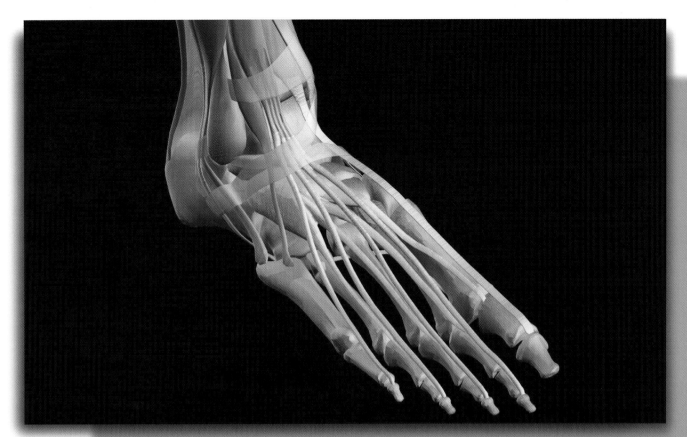

Stress fractures in the foot bones are the most common injuries among sprinters and hurdlers.

you and your doctor to figure out what caused the fracture in the first place so that you don't repeat the same mistake.

When you can walk normally and there's no tenderness in the area of the fracture, you can begin a gradual return to your sport. If you had to stop running, for instance, you might start out with long walks, then jogging, and then return to your normal running pace.

Stress fractures of the foot generally require a non-weight-bearing cast for at least six weeks. After that an additional six-week rehabilitation program follows to strengthen the area and give a gradual return to the sport.

ACL (anterior cruciate ligament—part of your knee) injuries, when the ligament tears, are particularly high for women involved in jumping sports. One cause is landing with a straight leg (with your knee locked). Learning to flex your knee when landing will help prevent this injury. Depending upon the severity of the tear, treatment can range from rest and immobilization to an operation to repair the tear. Recuperation time can last from five or six weeks to months if you've had surgery.

The shoulder joint sustains injury in sports involving overhand actions like throwing. The most common is an irritation of the rotator cuff and the surrounding soft tissue. Some of the symptoms of shoulder injury are a numbing pain throughout the arm, unusual sounds (like cracking or popping) when you rotate your shoulder, pain when doing something simple like throwing a ball, and an inability to raise your arm above 90 degrees. One theory why shoulder injuries are more common in female athletes is that they are not encouraged to strengthen their upper bodies, and thus, their shoulder muscles are not prepared to take physical stress.

Treatment depends on the severity of the injury. You might be given a painkiller or anti-inflammatory (something that reduces muscle swelling) drug, or even a shot of cortisone (a prescription anti-inflammatory drug). Shoulder injuries require a lot of rest—anywhere from eight weeks up. You should also get a rehabilitation program that involves progressive strengthening of the area to help you regain full use and movement in your shoulder.

Hamstring (the muscle on the back of your thigh) injuries are often seen in track and field athletes because many of the events require quick bursts of speed. Not warming up properly, being tired, and having poor flexibility all contribute to these injuries. Luckily, the majority can be treated through RICE—rest, ice, compression, and elevation. Putting an elastic wrap around the area can help reduce swelling, and a painkiller like acetaminophen (e.g., Tylenol) should alleviate any discomfort. If you're still in pain, see your doctor. Unfortunately, it takes a while to recover from any hamstring injury and the recurrence is high.

Runners often encounter sharp pains along the front or inside of the lower leg. These are called shin splints and are the result of muscle and tendon weakness caused by any number of factors, including increasing mileage too quickly, running on hard surfaces, or downhill running. Shin splints can be treated with rest, ice, and anti-inflammatory medications such as Advil. Prevention comes through strengthening the muscles of the lower leg and avoiding overtraining.

Overtraining

As a teen, you encounter a lot of pressure. Maybe your parents want you to succeed in track and field, maybe your classmates don't think you have what it takes, or maybe you doubt yourself. The desire to prove yourself can be a strong force in overtraining. Between school teams, personal trainers, and summer sports camps, you can find yourself training year-round.

While training regularly is vital for health and performance, your body needs rest to avoid fatigue and injury.

When you overtrain, your body has no time to recover. You start to fatigue (wear down) muscles and leave yourself open to injury. Frustrated, you ignore your body's warning signs—missed periods, chronic pain, and even decreased performance. Overtraining can be as detrimental as an injury.

The best way to recuperate is to rest. You don't have to be totally inactive, but take a break from track and field and try something different and less stressful, such as swimming or yoga. Gradually come back to your training, but increase your intensity slowly or you can risk reinjury.

Many injuries can be avoided through proper training and technique. You don't want to have to sit out a meet just because you didn't warm up properly when you went for a training run the other day, nor do you want to risk a shoulder injury because you're afraid lifting weights will make you big or bulky.

Listen to your body. Take it easy if you've had a tough workout and are tired. It doesn't make you a better athlete if you play through pain because in the end you and your team will suffer even more from your absence at the meet.

The Mental Game

Track and field isn't just about the physical. In order to excel, you need to work on your mental game as well. Perhaps the most important aspect of this is attitude. The difference between being a negative person and having a positive attitude can be the difference between performing poorly and performing well.

Sometimes it's hard not to beat yourself up over your performance and it feels impossible to be positive. In these times, having a phrase that gives you confidence can be a great help. Try saying something like, "If I don't give up, then I've already succeeded." Or if you're tired, just tell yourself, "I'm almost there, I can do it."

Focus is also important. If you have goals for yourself, such as finishing a race in a certain time or jumping a specific height, focusing on these will help you achieve them, keeping you motivated.

If you're having difficulty with your event, it often helps to think about it—to visualize it. Professional athletes use visualization techniques to help them perform better. For example, if you're nervous about knocking over the hurdles, imagine your perfect race. What would it look like? One of the benefits of visualization is that you can slow down, repeat, or even stop the action in your head. You can see yourself at the beginning of the race, your powerful start, your approach to the hurdle, and your follow-through. Visualization helps you to learn the event mentally, which makes it easier to put it into practice physically.

Nutrition

There's nothing worse than "bonking" (running out of energy) at a critical moment because you decided that one cheese danish would last you all day. To participate in a track and field meet that might keep you active for most of the day, you need to provide the proper fuel for your body.

A general rule for a young athlete is to get around 60 percent of your diet from carbohydrates. If you're a long-distance runner, you might increase that to 75 percent. "Carbs" come not only from pasta and breads, but fruits and vegetables as well.

Visualization techniques can help you "see" yourself winning an event. These techniques may assist you to mentally prepare for a competition.

Athletes need to eat good food to perform well. The United States Department
of Agriculture's food pyramid can be your guide to following a healthy diet.

Athletes generally require more protein than the average individual because of the muscle built during training. Protein also provides long-term energy, vitamins, and minerals. It also helps to repair tissue. Protein comes from animal sources—meat, cheese, and fish—and nonanimal sources, such as tofu and other soy products.

Fats are necessary in everyone's diet but they shouldn't contribute more than 30 percent of your daily calories. Many athletes choose a low-fat diet, which keeps their intake to between 10 and 15 percent. However, remember that your body is still developing. Check with your doctor before changing your diet.

Calcium is very important for young women, particularly since they don't often get enough of it from their regular diet. Calcium helps prevent osteoporosis, which can affect the young just as easily as the old. Calcium supplements can ensure that you get the recommended dosage of between 1,200 and 1,500 milligrams a day.

Scheduling your eating around your meet is a good strategy. Figure out what works best for your body. Do you do well eating an English muffin with peanut butter an hour before your event, or is it better to have an egg and some toast three hours before? Don't experiment on the day of a meet! Most athletes like to eat something one to four hours before their event. It's also good to eat something right after an event, since your muscles need to take in more fuel at that time.

Make sure you drink lots of water before, during, and after your competition. Dehydration can be a serious issue and water helps keep your system functioning smoothly. Some endurance athletes, like long-distance runners, will often have a sports drink during their race as well.

Unfortunately, images in magazines and on television reinforce the ideal of a thin young woman. Track and field uniforms can be revealing, making some girls feel self-conscious. A girl's unhealthy preoccupation with weight can result in the female athlete triad—a combination of eating disorders (like bulimia or anorexia), low bone density, and missed periods. Sometimes athletes become obsessed with controlling their weight because they can't control the outcome of their games. Being healthy and strong is one of the most important things for an athlete. Eating disorders destroy that.

Performance Enhancing Drugs

Not just Olympic and professional athletes experiment with performance enhancing (ergogenic) aids. An increasing number of young athletes are also seduced by the promise of an extra performance edge. Two of the most common drugs are anabolic steroids and creatine.

Anabolic steroids are an artificial version of testosterone, the male hormone. Female athletes have used them to gain muscle mass and lose fat. Between the 1970s and 1990s, some Olympic athletes from China and the former East Germany used them. Steroids are now banned from the Olympics, but some athletes still use them during training.

Unfortunately, there isn't sufficient information on the effects of long-term and repeated use.

Creatine is a commercially available supplement. A natural substance found in raw meat and fish, it is important for high-intensity muscle contractions. It appears to be widely used among sprinters. Like caffeine, it does not seem to affect lengthy exercise. Studies indicate that it does benefit quick bursts of all-out effort like sprinting; however, the long-term effects on the heart and kidneys are still unknown.

If you feel that your diet is lacking an important element, then talk to your doctor or a nutritionist. It's better to get your competitive edge from food rather than drugs.

3

Competition

Track and field is both an individual and a team sport. Individuals participate in each event but come to the meet (and train) as members of a team. Athletes are scored on their individual performances but sometimes are also awarded points that are tallied for a team score. Meets like the Olympics only keep individual scores (but everyone likes to keep a medal count for their country). National meets among colleges and universities are team scored. How many points an individual performance receives varies from meet to meet.

Meets can take place at indoor or outdoor tracks, permitting a longer competition season. The indoor track season usually lasts from January through March and most schools and colleges have track seasons that last throughout the school year.

Running events can be held year round. Cross-country (long-distance) events are usually held in the fall in the United States, while the international community holds them in the winter. The United States and Canada move track and field indoors during the winter. Sometimes this causes events to be eliminated or modified because of space considerations.

School and club meets are generally one-day events. Larger championship events often need at least two days. Many field events have qualifying rounds. At smaller meets, participants have three tries at each event with the top six to nine finishers moving onto the next round. Larger meets add an additional round to accommodate the larger number of participants.

Competition is a healthy aspect of sports, as well as of life, as long as you keep it in perspective. This means realizing that it is not all under your control. You might have an off day; many athletes do. It's important to keep your focus on how you perform rather than on the outcome of a competition.

Get enough rest on the night before a meet. Also, taper off your training right before the event. That means cutting back to have enough energy left for the meet.

Team Play

Not only do you go to meets with the same team of athletes, you sometimes compete against each other as well. It's okay to beat your teammate at an event. When you get out on the

Track and field offers a combination of individual and team activities.
Individuals participate in each event but train and compete as a team.

If you are encountering poor sportsmanship or bad behavior from members of your own team or from your competitors, it might help to seek advice from your coach.

track or step into the launching circle, you can only focus on your own performance. Sometimes, unfortunately, feelings get hurt and your teammate might be angry. Let her know that you were only doing your best, not focusing on beating her. Clear communication and understanding help build a better team.

Good Sportswomanship

It's easy to get caught up in competition and forget how you're behaving. Taunting rival athletes or trying to distract a jumper before she takes off are examples of poor sportswomanship. Mocking another team or athlete doesn't help your performance; it just makes you look bad.

If there is trouble between your team and another, the best thing to do is just walk away. Fighting or being belligerent doesn't make a loss easier or a victory sweeter.

4 Opportunities for Track and Field Athletes

Women in sports are gaining more and more recognition, and many spectators show up for the championship track and field meets that are held each year. Girls don't have to see their athletic careers end after college or the Olympics, and they don't have to choose between sports and academics, either. Sports scholarships are offered at schools across the country, from Ivy League schools to state universities.

Many athletes become coaches for schools and universities. Others become personal trainers who focus on one or two athletes. There are many options available to you.

You don't have to be a professional athlete to continue competing as an adult. There are plenty of recreational clubs for adults, and some of the resources at the back of this book will help you find teams. Just because they aren't "elite" doesn't mean a lack of competition or commitment to the sport, so you don't have to worry about losing your edge. A love of the game developed now can last well into your adult life.

The benefits of fitness and the love of competition can help you in all areas of your life. A strong and healthy mind and body is something you can develop through participation in track and field. There is an event for every kind of athlete. Go out there and find yours.

Track and field offers events for every kind of athlete.

Javelins

Track Shoes

Hurdle

Shot Put

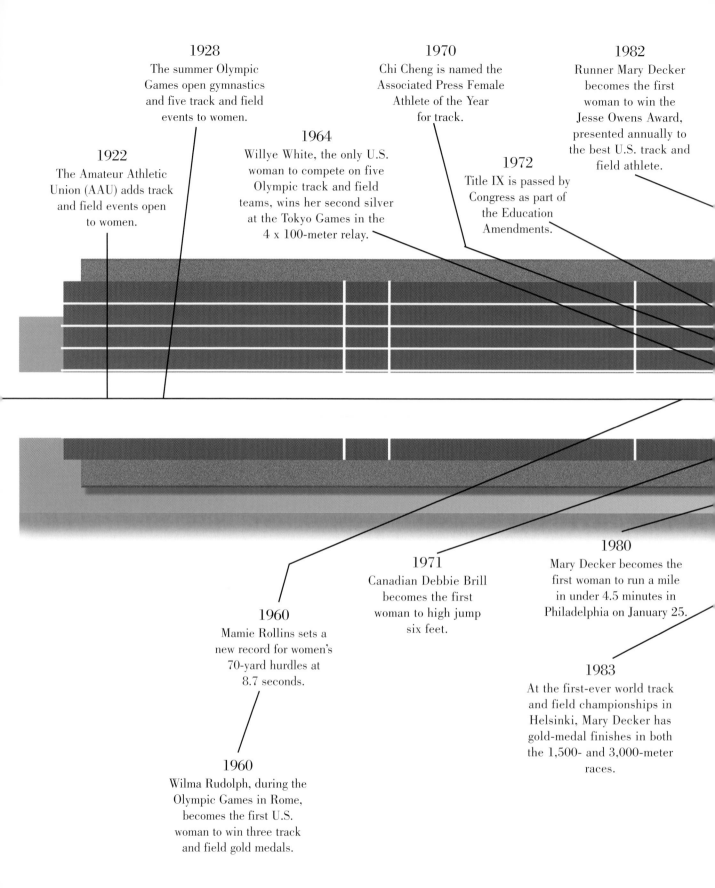

1928
The summer Olympic Games open gymnastics and five track and field events to women.

1970
Chi Cheng is named the Associated Press Female Athlete of the Year for track.

1982
Runner Mary Decker becomes the first woman to win the Jesse Owens Award, presented annually to the best U.S. track and field athlete.

1922
The Amateur Athletic Union (AAU) adds track and field events open to women.

1964
Willye White, the only U.S. woman to compete on five Olympic track and field teams, wins her second silver at the Tokyo Games in the 4 x 100-meter relay.

1972
Title IX is passed by Congress as part of the Education Amendments.

1971
Canadian Debbie Brill becomes the first woman to high jump six feet.

1980
Mary Decker becomes the first woman to run a mile in under 4.5 minutes in Philadelphia on January 25.

1960
Mamie Rollins sets a new record for women's 70-yard hurdles at 8.7 seconds.

1983
At the first-ever world track and field championships in Helsinki, Mary Decker has gold-medal finishes in both the 1,500- and 3,000-meter races.

1960
Wilma Rudolph, during the Olympic Games in Rome, becomes the first U.S. woman to win three track and field gold medals.

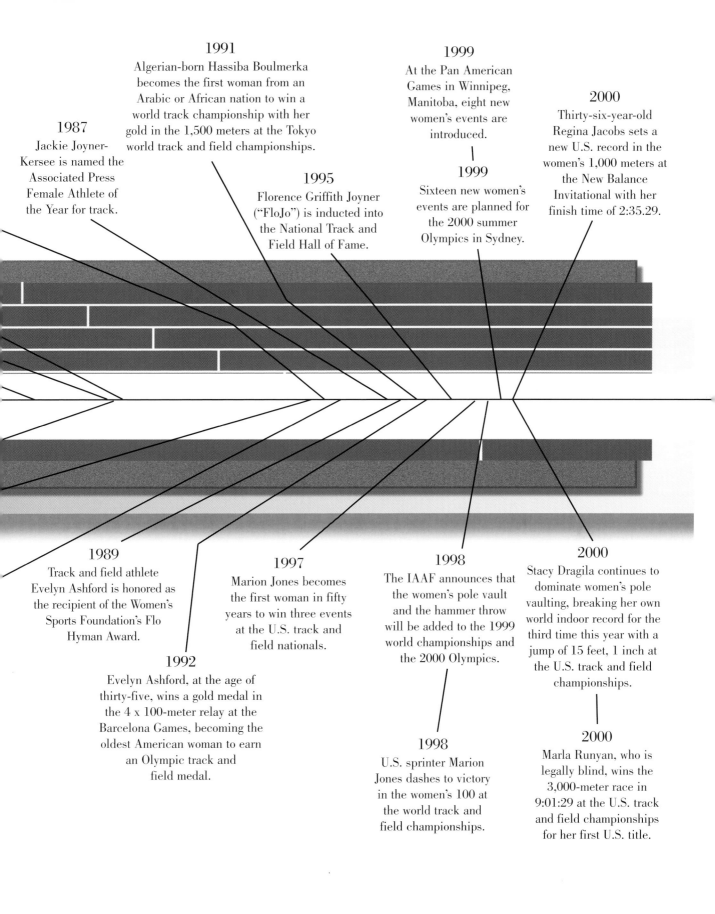

1987
Jackie Joyner-Kersee is named the Associated Press Female Athlete of the Year for track.

1991
Algerian-born Hassiba Boulmerka becomes the first woman from an Arabic or African nation to win a world track championship with her gold in the 1,500 meters at the Tokyo world track and field championships.

1995
Florence Griffith Joyner ("FloJo") is inducted into the National Track and Field Hall of Fame.

1999
At the Pan American Games in Winnipeg, Manitoba, eight new women's events are introduced.

1999
Sixteen new women's events are planned for the 2000 summer Olympics in Sydney.

2000
Thirty-six-year-old Regina Jacobs sets a new U.S. record in the women's 1,000 meters at the New Balance Invitational with her finish time of 2:35.29.

1989
Track and field athlete Evelyn Ashford is honored as the recipient of the Women's Sports Foundation's Flo Hyman Award.

1992
Evelyn Ashford, at the age of thirty-five, wins a gold medal in the 4 x 100-meter relay at the Barcelona Games, becoming the oldest American woman to earn an Olympic track and field medal.

1997
Marion Jones becomes the first woman in fifty years to win three events at the U.S. track and field nationals.

1998
The IAAF announces that the women's pole vault and the hammer throw will be added to the 1999 world championships and the 2000 Olympics.

1998
U.S. sprinter Marion Jones dashes to victory in the women's 100 at the world track and field championships.

2000
Stacy Dragila continues to dominate women's pole vaulting, breaking her own world indoor record for the third time this year with a jump of 15 feet, 1 inch at the U.S. track and field championships.

2000
Marla Runyan, who is legally blind, wins the 3,000-meter race in 9:01:29 at the U.S. track and field championships for her first U.S. title.

Glossary

agility   The ability to move quickly and easily.

anorexia   An eating disorder that involves compulsive dieting and extreme thinness.

baton   A hollow cylinder passed from one member of a relay team to another.

bulimia   Compulsive overeating followed by self-induced vomiting.

heptathalon   A track and field competition comprised of seven events.

ligament   The band of tissue that connects bones and holds organs together.

osteoporosis   Bone density loss resulting in brittle bones.

pace/pacing   To run at the speed that allows you to complete a course successfully.

taunt/taunting   To mock, make fun or, or insult.

tendon   The tissue that connects muscle to bone.

For More Information

In the United States

Road Runners Club of America
510 North Washington Square
Alexandria, VA 22314
(703) 836-0558
e-mail: office@rrca.org
Web site: http://www.rrca.org

USA Track and Field
P.O. Box 120
Indianapolis, IN 46206-0120
(317) 261-0500
  e-mail: dhtrack@aol.com
    Web site: http://usatf.org

In Canada

Athletics Canada
Suite 606
1185 Eglinton Avenue East
Toronto, ON M3C 3C6
e-mail: athcan@athletics.ca
Web site: http://www.athleticscanada.com

Web Sites

Girls on the Run
http://www.girlsontherun.com

I-Glow For Girls Who Play
http://www.i-glow.com

Jackie Joyner-Kersee Boys and Girls Club
http://www.jjkbgc.org

For Further Reading

Bailey, Donna. *Track and Field*. Austin, TX: Steck-Vaughn Library, 1991.

Blackall, Bernie. *Track and Field*. Des Plaines, IL: Heinemann Library, 1999.

Crawford, Terry, and Bob Bertucci. *Winning Track and Field Drills for Women*. West Point, NY: Leisure Press, 1985.

Foreman, Ken. *Coaching Track and Field Techniques*. 4th ed. Dubuque, IA: W.C. Brown Co., 1982.

Hughes, Morgan E. *Track and Field*. Vero Beach, FL: Rourke Press, 2001.

Macht, Norman L. *The Composite Guide to Track and Field*. Philadelphia, PA: Chelsea House Publishers, 1999.

Marx, Doug. *Track and Field*. Vero Beach, FL.: Rourke Press, 1994.

McMane, Fred. *Track and Field Basics*. Englewood Cliffs, NJ: Prentice-Hall, 1983.

Page, Jason. *Athletics, Field: Pole Vault, Long Jump, Hammer, Javelin, and Lots, Lots More*. Minneapolis, MN: LernerSports, 2000.

Page, Jason. *Athletics, Track: 100 Meters, 200 Meters, Relays, Hurdles, and Lots, Lots More*. Minneapolis, MN: LernerSports, 2000.

Potts, Steve. *Track and Field*. Mankato, MN: Creative Education, 1993.

Rosenthal, Bert. *Track and Field*. Austin, TX: Raintree Steck-Vaughn, 1994.

Rudolph, Wilma. *Wilma Rudolph on Track*. New York: Wanderer Books, 1980.

Rutledge, Rachel. *Women of Sports: The Best of the Best in Track and Field*. Brookfield, CT: Millbrook Press, 1999.

Sabin, Louis. *Run Faster, Jump Higher, Throw Farther: How to Win at Track and Field*. New York: Davis McKay, 1980.

Santos, Jim, and Ken Shannon. *Sports Illustrated Track: The Field Events*. New York: Sports Illustrated, 1999.

Smale, David. *Track and Field*. Mankato, MN: Smart Apple Media, 1995.

Sullivan, George. *Better Field Events for Girls*. New York: Dodd, Mead, 1982.

Sullivan, George. *Better Track for Girls*. New York: Dodd, Mead, 1981.

Tricard, Louise Mead. *American Women's Track and Field: A History, 1895 Through 1980*. Jefferson, NC: McFarland & Co., 1996.

Ward, Tony. *Track and Field*. Crystal Lake, IL: Rigby Interactive Library, 1997.

Wright, Gary. *Track and Field: A Step-by-Step Guide*. Mahwah, NJ: Troll Associates, 1990.

Zadra, Dan. *Track and Field Warming Up*. Mankato, MN: Children's Book Co., 1981.

Index

A

academics, 47
ACL injuries, 32
Athletics Canada, 11

B

baton, 16
belly flop, 18

C

caffeine, 41
Callipateira, 5
cardiovascular training, 21–22
Civil Rights Restoration Act, 8
coaches, 47
competition, healthy, 43–46, 48

creatine, 40, 41
cross-country events, 12
cross training, 29
cycling, 29–30

D

dehydration, 39–40
discus throwing, 10, 12, 16
Dragila, Stacy, 18
drugs, performance enhancing, 40

E

eating disorders, 40
equipment and cost, 11–12, 30
ergogenic drugs, 40

F

fatigue, 34–35, 36
female athlete triad, 40
field events, 16–20, 43
Fosbury, Dick, 18
Fosbury flop, 18

G

goals, 36
Grove City v. Bell, 7

H

hammer throwing, 7, 10, 12, 16,
    19–20
hamstring injuries, 33
heptathalon, 10, 20
high jump, 10, 16–18, 20
hurdles/hurdling, 10, 15, 36

I

indoor track, 11, 42, 43
injuries, 30–33, 34, 35
International Amateur Athletic
    Federation, 7

J

javelin, 10, 11, 16

L

long-distance runs, 14, 15, 36, 40, 43
long jump, 16, 18

M

marathon running, 5, 10, 15, 21
mental game, 35
mid-distance runs, 14

N

New York Athletic Club, 7
nutrition/diet, 30, 36–40, 41

O

Olympic Games, 5, 6, 7, 9, 15, 16,
    18, 40, 47
    2000 Sydney Olympics, 16, 18, 20
osteoporosis/low bone density, 23,
    30, 39, 40
outdoor track, 11, 42
overtraining, 33–35

P

pacing, 14
periods, missed, 40
pole vault, 10, 11, 16, 18
positive attitude, 35–36

R

race walking, 10, 16
relays, 10, 16
RICE, 33

S

scholarships, 47

scissors, 18

scoring, 42

sex discrimination, 7–8

shin splints, 33

shoes, 11

shot put, 5, 10, 12, 16, 19, 20

shoulder injuries, 32

Skolimowska, Kamila, 20

sports camps, 33

sprinting, 12–13, 14, 21, 30, 41

starting blocks, 13

steeplechase, 15–16

steroids, anabolic, 40–41

strength/weight training, 22–26,
      30, 35

stress fractures, 30–31

stretching/warming up,
      26–28, 35

T

Tailteann Games, 5

Title IX, 7–9

track and field, early days, 6, 7

track events, 12–16

track season, 42–43

trainer, 5, 33, 47

triple jump, 10, 16, 18

U

USA Track and Field, 11

V

visualization, 36

W

water jump, 15

weight, 40

western roll, 18

Y

yoga, 30

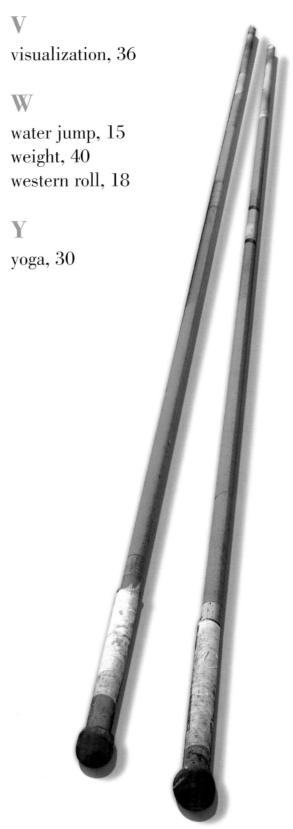

About the Author

Claudia B. Manley is an author who lives in New York with her son, partner, and cat.

Credits

Cover photo by Maura Boruchow; pp. 3, 10, 11,14, 15, 19, 21, 22, 24, 27, 34, 42, 44, 47, 49, 50, 51, 54, 56, 55, 57, 58, 61, 63 by Maura Boruchow; p. 6 © Archivo Iconografico, S.A./Corbis; p. 8 © AP/Worldwide; p. 12 © Agence Vandystadt/Allsport; p. 13, 50 © Corbis; p. 17 © Mike Powell/Allsport; pp. 29, 37 © FPG International; p. 31 © LifeArt; p. 38 © Leonard Lessin/Peter Arnold, Inc.; p. 45 © Superstock. Diagrams on pp. 4, 52–53 by Tom Forget.

Special thanks to Cardinal Gibbons High School in Fort Lauderdale, Florida.

Series Design

Danielle Goldblatt

Layout

Claudia Carlson